T0364117

Life Word

discover your
one word
to leave a legacy

ON GORDON   DAN BRITTON   JIMMY PAGE

WILEY

contents

Foreword

My *Life Word*? **Potential**.

In a sentence, my life purpose is to help others maximize their God-given potential. That's true whether I'm pastoring, parenting, or writing. I believe in dreaming big, praying hard, and thinking long. I believe that obstacles are opportunities to stretch our faith and grow stronger. I believe in praying like it depends on God and working like it depends on us. And I believe that God is ordering our footsteps and preparing good works in advance. In other words, I live my life with a profound sense of destiny. And you can, too! This book will help!

A few years ago, I started an annual tradition of choosing a word for the year after reading *One Word That Will Change Your Life* by Jon Gordon, Dan Britton, and Jimmy Page. It was a game changer for me. *Life Word* takes that revolutionary idea to the next level. What Jon, Dan, and Jimmy have discovered and share with you in this book is a simple, powerful, and life-changing idea that really works.

When you discover your *Life Word*—that one word that defines you and drives you to be your best and make a difference in this world—you'll live with more clarity and confidence than ever before. And as you trust God to do the impossible in your life, you'll take powerful steps toward living your destiny and leaving a legacy that truly matters.

I don't want to waste a single day. I want to wake up in the morning and live with a sense of passion as I pursue God's biggest dreams for my life. I refuse to be derailed by doubt or frustrated by fear. And so should you!

Don't just *read* this book. Dig into it. And when you discover your *Life Word*, don't look back! It won't just change you; I believe you'll change the world because of it.

Mark Batterson
New York Times best-selling author
of *Chase the Lion* and *The Circle Maker*

Introduction

Living deep within the heart of every person is a passion and desire to live a life that truly matters. We want to make a positive contribution and make a difference. We want to live in such a way that the world is better because we were here. Ultimately, we want to leave a positive legacy that lives on long after we're gone.

In this book we reveal a simple, powerful tool to help you do just that! It's found in just a single word—One Word to leave a legacy. We call this One Word a *Life Word*.

The following pages guide you step-by-step to discover your *Life Word*. This *Life Word* helps you leave a legacy that truly makes a difference in this world and in the lives of others. It's your One Word vision for your life that inspires you to live your best life and make your greatest impact.

Your *Life Word* gives you the desire and direction to live your destiny.

It's a proven way to create more clarity, confidence, and courage for living a life that matters. Discovering your *Life Word* gives you a compelling vision for the future; it helps you align your priorities, energy, and actions behind your purpose and passion. It helps you see the big picture and maintain a long-term focus for your life. By focusing on this simple word you will avoid distractions, stay on track, and live with fewer regrets. It's all about living with the end in mind.

Your *Life Word* creates more clarity, confidence, and courage.

To help you discover your *Life Word*, we've created a simple, three-part process:

1. **Define your Power.** This step helps you identify your gifts and strengths. You've been blessed with distinct abilities that make you unique and special. This is answering the "Who" question—*Who are you meant to be?*

2. **Determine your Purpose.** This helps uncover your direction. We have a certain mission and work that has our name on it. It reveals the difference you desire to make in the world. This is answering the "Why" question—*Why are you here?*
3. **Discover your Passion.** This uncovers your desire. It's what motivates and inspires you. It reveals your heart and helps move your focus to how you will positively influence others. This is answering the "What" question—*What energizes you?*

We've also created an action plan featured at the end of the book to help you implement and maximize the *Life Word* process so that you can live on purpose and build a legacy that lasts.

This book is the perfect companion to our book *One Word That Will Change Your Life* where we revealed the process to discover the One Word that is meant for you each year. This One Word for the year helps you live in the present and experience incredible life change. One Word creates a short-term focus that leads to long-term impact. Each word for each year completes a chapter in your life story. Your character and your actions will be shaped and you will become the person you were made to be. Leaving a lasting legacy and the mark of impact requires living out your word each year.

The response from *One Word That Will Change Your Life* has been amazing—more than 100,000 books sold and more than 500,000 subscriptions to our four-day reading plan with YouVersion. There are hundreds of thousands of One Word fanatics who have experienced an incredible transformation from living their One Word each year. But we have discovered that One Word is just a part of the story. Discovering and living your *Life Word* is the rest.

The One Word to leave a legacy process helps you begin with the end in mind and stay focused on the future by helping you find your *Life Word*. We all end up somewhere, but so few seem to end up there on purpose. Your *Life Word* keeps you focused on the long term and the impact you hope to have on others. This *Life Word* is the title of your life story.

Begin with the end in mind.

Not only will your life be marked as you live your *Life Word*, but more importantly, others will be impacted. The real power is the transformation that takes place not only in you but also through you.

Ordinary men and women over the years who have lived with power, purpose, and passion have left enduring legacies and have changed the world. It's fun to consider what their possible *Life Words* would be:

For Martin Luther King Jr., was it *Equality?*
Mother Theresa's was undoubtedly *Compassion.*
Abraham Lincoln's could have been *Unite.*
Helen Keller's was probably *Vision.*
George Washington's was most likely *Lead.*
Jackie Robinson's may have been *Breakthrough.*
William Wallace's legacy may be *Freedom.*
Susan B. Anthony's was probably *Vote.*
And perhaps the greatest *Life Word* was Jesus's legacy of *Love.*

As we take you on this journey to find your *Life Word*, think about possible words that you stand for and might define you. This word will ultimately help shape your destiny and maybe even history! You are the next great generation of history-makers. What will your *Life Word* be?

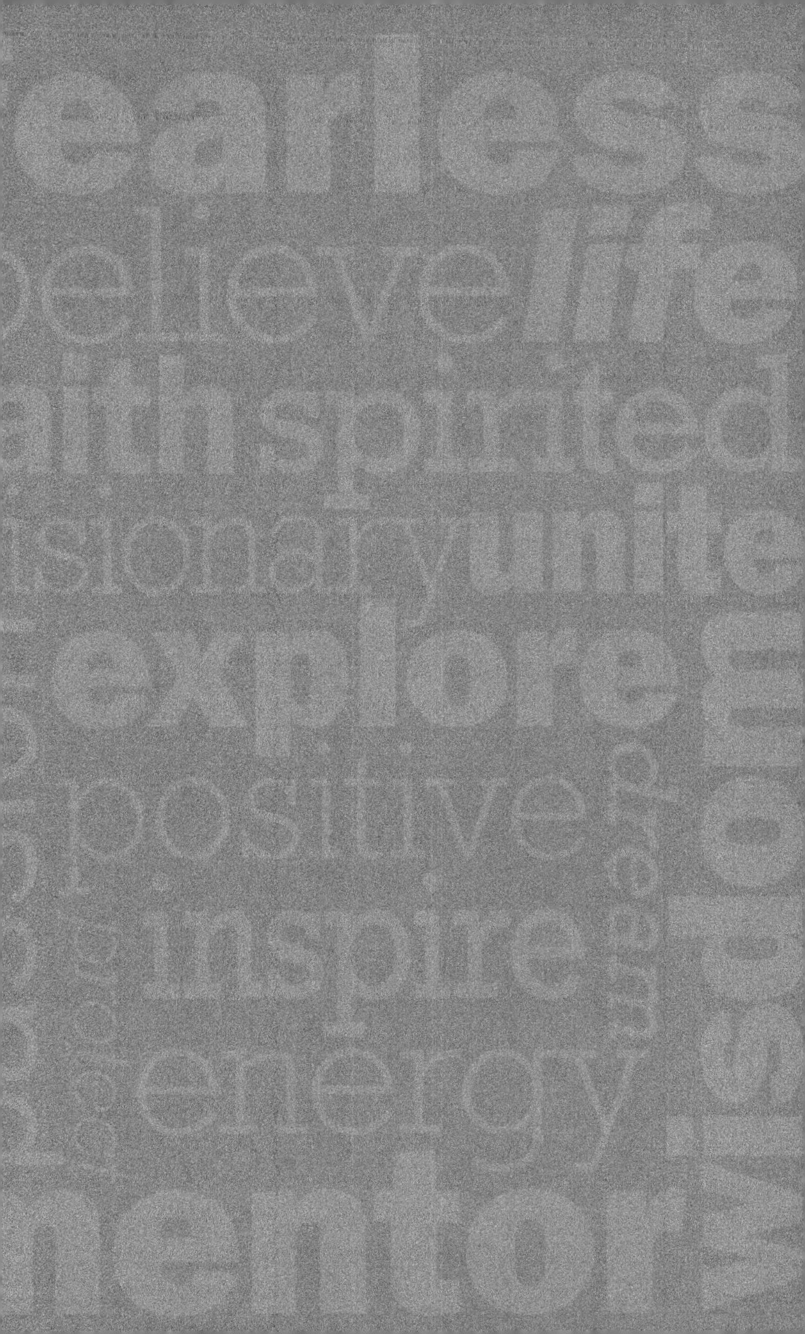
explore
positive
inspire
energy

fearless
believe lif
faith spirite
visionary uni
explore
passion positive
inspire
energy
mentor

chapter 1

The Story of *Life Word*

In the movie *Secondhand Lions***,** Walter, a 12-year-old boy, is dropped off with his "crazy uncles," Hub and Garth, for the summer. This turns into a wild ride of discovery. Legend has it that his uncles have lived an incredible life of adventure, victory, and defeat, love and loss, and great fortune. But rumors swirl that they are bank robbers or even worse and that they are sitting on top of millions.

The movie unfolds with unbelievable tales of adventure as the young boy tries to determine what and who to believe in. Along the way he is raised by and comes to love his valiant, heroic uncles and learns first-hand what it takes be a man and live life to the fullest. The final scene culminates with the uncles dying at the age of 90 as they try to fly a plane upside down through a barn.

As Walter arrived at the barn he met up with the grandson of a sheik who had been part of the epic tales. There he was asked, "So these men from the stories really *lived*?" To which he responded, "Yes, they *really* lived."

That's what *Life Word* is all about—ensuring that we *really* live.

When we're young, we have big dreams about changing the world and pursuing greatness. We are told that we can "be whoever we want to be" and we can "do great things," but inevitably the reality of life—the responsibilities and stress and busyness—often distracts us from our dreams and robs us of our sense of purpose and passion. We begin to lose focus on what is possible, what we're made for, and what we're passionate about. We settle for the "easy" road. We often become complacent and play it safe. We're directed by the expectations of others instead of our God-given purpose and path. And worst of all, we lose sight of that vision to use our unique gifts and talents to make this world a better place and leave a lasting legacy.

Australian nurse Bronnie Ware spent several years caring for terminal patients in the last 12 weeks of life. Her patients experienced a phenomenal clarity of vision as they neared death that we must learn from. From this experience she compiled a list of the top five regrets of the dying. The number one regret that people shared when looking back on their lives was—*I didn't live the life I was made to live.* Somewhere along the line they got off track and had lost sight of the vision they had for their life. They described countless unfulfilled dreams and knew it was due to choices they had made; they took their eyes off their purpose and lived a life others expected of them instead of pursuing their dreams.

By helping you discover your *Life Word*, we give you a telescope to see far into the future of your life. We help you discover your unique purpose and path. And you'll choose a *Life Word* that will help you stay on track and live a life of impact. In the end you'll make a mark that makes a difference and you'll pass on a legacy worth leaving behind.

We've all heard it said that life is short. It's like a vapor that appears and is gone; it's like the steam that rises from the pot of tea. Or the morning fog that settles just above the ground, but quickly disappears with the rising sun. And because it's short, we are compelled to make the most of it!

Life is short. Make the most of it!

Discovering your *Life Word* changes your perspective entirely. It helps you begin with the end in mind, see the big picture, and discover the purpose of your life. It's discovered at the intersection of the answers to three big three questions—Who, Why, and What:

Who am I made to be? Why am I here? What energizes me?

And, it captures all of that into a single *Life Word* to help you navigate true north and live a life that leaves an impact. No matter what stage of life you are in, your *Life Word* will help you discover your purpose, maximize your opportunities, and leave a positive, lasting legacy.

Our own experience with this process has been transformational. We'd like to share our stories with you.

Dan's Story

When I think of legacy, I think of one person . . . my father. He was an incredible man who lived well and died well. He passed away in 2008, but his legacy lives on because he lived life with passion, enthusiasm, and intensity. Battling leukemia for 18 months, he was still focused on finishing well, fighting the good fight, and running the right race. Days before dying, he wrote in his journal, "I'm absolutely convinced that I'm able to stay positive due to the ongoing prayers of all of you! I am enjoying daily the final laps of my life." He lived life to its fullest—to the very end.

My dad lived every second of the day as if it were his last. Not just when he became sick, but throughout his entire life. His favorite quote was, "Life is God's gift to us. What we do with it is our gift back to Him." That became his life's ambition. He made an impact on everyone around him and you never forgot Ed Britton.

Live each day like it's your last.

As a result of the legacy he lived . . . and left, I discovered my *Life Word*. I realized that my motivation is to live every day as if it were my last. To show up with everything I have and pour out my life every single second, minute, hour, day, week, month, and year. I want to count every day so that I make every day count.

My *Life Word* is **Passion**. I desire to infuse life into every circumstance, every meeting, every relationship, and every encounter. It's about living life with reckless abandonment. When it is all said and done, I want someone to say about me, "Dan was passionate about God and passionate about others."

Jimmy's Story

I've always loved rooting for the underdog. And I love the big upset when the team with little to no chance of winning actually makes it happen! Heck, I loved being the underdog.

Being the smallest kid in my class until I was a junior in high school made me work super hard to compete against the bigger kids. I would get home from school, put down my books, pick up a ball, and go to work; I put in thousands of hours of extra work just to be my best on the courts or fields. I did it because I loved it. I was routinely underestimated and it fueled me to be my best.

Growing up playing Little League baseball, our team was from the town that didn't splurge on full uniforms, so when we played in tournaments, we looked like a ragtag, mismatched bunch! That made it even more exciting when we would walk away with the trophy as our opponents shook their heads in disbelief.

I love gritty inspirational movies like *Rocky*, *Miracle*, *Rudy*, and *October Sky*—the ones that show us what's possible with enough hard work, passion, and persistence. The movies that inspire you to dream bigger dreams, take bigger risks, and believe in the impossible; to overcome incredible obstacles and challenges and face your fears.

Dream bigger dreams, take bigger risks, believe in the impossible.

I love the stories of superheroes and everyday heroes and I'm inspired by them. I've been inspired by my parents, teachers, coaches, those who have sacrificed in the military, and people on the streets. People who take a stand for what they believe or defend the defenseless—they inspire me, too. Even today, I want to be inspired and inspire others.

That's why my *Life Word* is **Inspire**. It burns in me to inspire others to explore and experience God's best for their life. This focuses and motivates me whenever I write, speak, or develop leaders and it influences every relationship and interaction. I want to live in such a way—using my gifts, passion, and platform—to inspire people to live life to the fullest.

Jon's Story

I'm not naturally positive. People think I am because of the books I write and talks that I give, but I have to work hard at it. I often joke that growing up in a Jewish, Italian family with a lot of food and a lot of guilt didn't help. In my late twenties after struggling with my own negativity, fear, and depression, I remember asking God why I was so miserable and what was I born to do?

Writing and speaking came to me and so did the mission of becoming more positive and sharing positivity with others. Over the years I realized my gifts were in teaching, communicating, writing, and inspiring. I found my purpose in teaching what I needed to learn and creating a more positive world, one person at a time. I discovered I'm passionate about helping leaders, organizations, teams, and people from all walks of life become more positive.

Creating a more positive world, one person at a time.

My daughter recently wrote her college admissions essay. She started it like this. "When I was young my mom struggled with her health and my dad struggled with himself. He was very negative and unhappy, but I watched as he worked to become a more positive person. Then he started writing and speaking and sharing positive messages with others. I saw how he changed and how other people changed. I know if he can change and they can change, the world can change." I teared up after reading her words, because I saw how my path of becoming more positive impacted my marriage, my children, my work, and those who read my books.

I know without a doubt that being positive not only makes you better, it makes everyone around you better. I know that **Positive** is my *Life Word*, calling, and mission. Every day I wake up I know my job is to live it and share it.

Your Story

Your *Life Word* gives you a simple, powerful reminder to make sure that you live on purpose, align your priorities, and live with passion to make a difference for others. It acts as a light-house of sorts to help you stay focused on the things that matter most.

We believe there is a *Life Word* that's meant for you. It's a word that captures who you are, why you're here, and what drives you. It captures your hopes and dreams mixed with your gifts and talents. It helps you live well and leave a legacy that you are designed to leave—a legacy that will change the world and make it better in some important way. What's your story?

fearless

believe life

faith spirited

visionary unite

explore

positive dream

inspire

energy

mentor vision

fearless

believe lif

faith spirite

visionaryunit

explore

positive

inspire

energy

mentor

chapter 2

The Significance of Legacy

It's been said that two things in life are certain—death and taxes. Most of us have experienced the loss of someone we know; eventually we all will. And at the funerals people will share memories about their loved ones and the impact they made in their life. Sometimes we leave inspired by the life that was lived as shared in those stories. Other times we leave empty or sad.

It's been said that two things in life are certain—death and taxes.

But every single time we attend a funeral it makes us stop and think about our own life. We may ask ourselves, "Am I the person I want to be? How am I living? Am I making a difference?" The answers to these powerful questions can serve to reinforce the path we are on or as a catalyst for reflection and life-change.

But perhaps the most challenging question we typically ask is this, "What will people say about me at my funeral?" It can be a scary question to consider, but in some ways it's the most important one to ask. For many, it's a wake-up call.

What will people say about me at my funeral?

When it's all said and done, what will people say? How will I have impacted their life? Is the way I am living right now going to result in the legacy I hope to leave in the lives of others? What mark will I make? All of the accomplishments and achievements will be relatively meaningless when compared to how your life has impacted those around you and the difference you have made.

We recently had a conversation with a high school coach who was working with a girls' team in East Asia. He met with one of the most talented players on the team who he believed had untapped potential. He asked her this simple question, "Why do you play?" She quickly replied, "I want to be famous." The coach then went to the white board, drew a tombstone, and wrote her word—**Famous**—on the tombstone.

He then asked her, "Is that the mark you want
to leave? Is that big enough? Is it important
enough? Is that what you want to be known
for? Will that make a difference for others?"
After a little more thought she said, "No.
I really want to inspire young girls so they
know they can overcome any adversity; they
can rise above their challenges and circumstances and make a better future. I want to
give young girls hope. That's why I play!" That
was a game-changer. The coach had helped
his athlete tap into her purpose and passion

and he knew that was the key to unlocking her potential.

What do you think her new *Life Word* would be? How might that change the way she approaches her life? That's the fun and power of discovering your One Word.

Far too few people live in the present with the future in mind. Some get stuck in the past, dwelling on failures or dreaming about what could have been. Others get caught up in the busyness of life and lose sight of their hopes and dreams. What's most important gets swallowed up by the pace of life and the tyranny of the urgent. We are so busy just trying to keep up with the demands of family and work that we don't take time to live on purpose.

Far too many people get stuck in the past or paralyzed in the present.

In the best-selling business book *7 Habits of Highly Effective People*, author Stephen Covey shares habit #2—begin with the end in mind. He shares the power of creating a clear vision or mental picture of a desired direction and destination. The clearer the vision, the more likely we are to achieve it.

Few people think about the end of their life or their funeral. Most of us don't talk about, think about, or consider the legacy that we're going to leave while we're living. We just let others talk about it after we're gone. Others reflect back on the mark that a person has left, but that person most likely had not lived intentionally with their legacy in mind.

Will I live well?

When you discover and are guided by your *Life Word*, it helps you consider what legacy you will leave before it's too late to shape it. What mark will you make? How will you live? Will you live well?

So let's discover our *Life Word* and refuse to waste our lives on things that don't really matter. Let's refuse to be distracted by meaningless busyness and to be weighed down by unchangeable regrets. Let's live on purpose for a purpose because we all have purpose.

Let's live well!

believe
faith
visionary
explore
positive
inspire
energy
mentor

chapter 3

The Power of Legacy

Legacy is all about people. It's defined by what you leave behind that lives on in others. Each one of us plays a number of roles in life and every role matters. Some of us have the role of spouse, parent, leader, friend, co-worker, neighbor, or volunteer. Ultimately, the value of your life and your legacy is revealed in the stories that those who were most important to you—those who knew you best—will tell.

Legacy is what you leave behind that lives on in others.

When we consider the most important roles we play and the impact we can have on people, we are motivated to live our best life. When we discover our *Life Word*, it gives us the focus we need to invest our time and energy in the things that matter most.

Our *Life Word* helps us maximize each role in life we play. We are able to keep our eyes on the vision for the future and the impact we can have in each role. As parents, we consider what our children will need—the character, mind-set, and skills—when they eventually leave home and chart their own course. As friends, we pay attention to ways we can encourage them to find and live on purpose. As spouses, we want to help our mates become their very best. In our work, we want to leave a piece of ourselves in everything we do, living with purpose to produce something of value.

No matter what role we play, our *Life Word* helps us maximize our opportunities and keep the end in mind.

For example, when working with leaders around the world, we often do a team-building exercise to help them define true success in life. The Retirement Party team builder is a way to take people out of their comfort zone and have them begin with the end in mind first. We want them to answer the question: *What do they want to be remembered for?*

When we get everyone seated at the beginning of our workshop, we let them know there is opportunity to honor a special person they all

know who is retiring. At this point, there is an
uneasiness among them and everyone begins
to look around the room wondering who it is.
Usually, there are one or two people in the
audience who are approaching retirement, but
nobody knows for sure who we are honoring.

What do you want to be remembered for?

Before we say who we are honoring, we show a
short movie clip from the comedy drama *About
Schmidt*. The clip shows Warren Schmidt, played
by Jack Nicholson, on his last day before retiring from a lifetime of service at World Insurance
Company. He is sitting at his desk staring at the
clock on the wall waiting for 5 o'clock to arrive.
As the seconds are ticking away, you notice
his almost empty office with just a few boxes
of personal stuff stacked neatly in the corner.
At exactly 5 o'clock, he gets up and grabs his
coat behind the door and before walking out, he
looks back into the office one last time, turns
off the lights, and then shuts the door.

We then turn to the audience and ask, "What was going on?" Right away, people comment how sad it was that nobody was there on his last day. How he was counting the seconds before retiring. They also share how depressing it is that he looked back into the office one last time before leaving, indicating regret.

We ask everyone to close their eyes and then we say "The person retiring is . . . you. This is your retirement party!" As they keep their eyes closed, we have them imagine a different ending, where co-workers, clients, family, friends, and loved ones have gathered to share the enormous impact that they have made in the lives of those who have assembled. We ask them to contemplate, "What stories are they telling about you? Listen deeply. What is the one thing you long for someone to say about you."

After several minutes, we tell them to open their eyes, because it is time to celebrate! We usually have plastic champagne glasses with sparkling cider so they can toast one another. We encourage them to go around the room to each person and briefly share the one thing they hoped to hear at their retirement party.

While "Celebrate" by Kool and the Gang is playing in the background, the room explodes with chatter, laughter, high-fives, hugs, and pure excitement. We then ask them to share something powerful they heard while about their impact. The responses are almost always the same:

He cared about others.

She loved me unconditionally.

My life is better because of her.

He cared more about his team than he did the results.

When people talk about legacy, it's all about making a difference for others.

We then ask what you did not hear, and those responses are also the same. Nobody shared about organizational success—how much profit they made, how many people they hired, how many hours they worked. When people begin to reflect on the legacy they want to leave, they talk about relationships and making a difference in the lives of others.

Ken Blanchard summarizes it best: "The journey of life is to move from a self-serving heart to a serving heart. You finally become an adult when you realize that life is about what you give, rather than what you get."

Legacy . . . "It's not about you!"

It's always about the lives we touch and the people we influence. It's about being our best and bringing out the best in others. It's not found in the selfish pursuit of greatness; it's found in serving others. If this exercise ever results in a preoccupation with ourselves, we've missed the point entirely. We are created to invest our lives for the benefit of others. When we begin with the end in mind, we see clearly what matters most. The power of legacy is your impact on others.

Life is about what you give, rather than what you get.

Your *Life Word* gets you focused on living and leaving a powerful legacy. It moves you from focusing on yourself to focusing on others. You move from being consumed with what you get in life to what you give in life. You realize you are a true success when you help others be successful.

Remember, the power of legacy is all about what you give, not what you get. Everyone leaves a legacy. Your *Life Word* will help you define, determine, and discover what you will leave behind.

earless
believe life
aith inspired
isionary unite
explore
positive
inspire
energy
nentor

chapter 4

The Process

Now that you can see the significance of legacy and the power of a focused life, it's time to go through the process of discovering your *Life Word*. We've developed a simple, yet powerful three-part process that provides an easy framework for finding your *Life Word*:

Step 1: *Define your Power* by identifying your gifts and strengths.

Step 2: *Determine your Purpose* by identifying your calling and cause.

Step 3: *Discover your Passion* by identifying your motivation and energy.

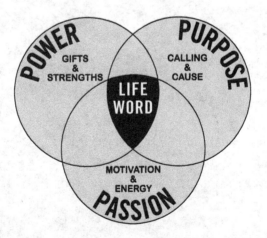

In the following chapters, we walk you through these components on your path to discovering your *Life Word*. We believe there is a word meant just for you that's found at the intersection of your power, passion, and purpose. We also know that it will positively impact every area of your life.

Life Word is for everyone who wants to make the most of their life. It's for those who realize that life is short and we only get one shot at it. It's for those who want to design and experience a life that fulfills its potential and truly makes a difference. It acts as a driving force to help you align all your energy and focus for the things that matter most. It helps you reduce clutter and eliminate distractions that keep you from your destiny.

Your *Life Word* becomes a driving force to align your efforts and eliminate distractions.

Everyone has the ability to select a *Life Word* that gives them direction and drive. It ultimately helps us live on purpose and stay on point. It helps us experience more mission and meaning. It helps us focus more on the important than the urgent. You will be amazed at how it helps you decide what to say "yes" and "no" to, keep the most important things in mind, and maximize your time and energy.

The process takes a little time, but the results will be worth it! So let's get started with the *Life Word* process.

chapter 5

Define
Your
Power

When the kids were little, they loved superheroes like Superman, Spiderman, Wonder Woman, and Captain America. It was fun to watch them use their imaginations and dream that they could be superheroes, too. We would occasionally ask them, "If you were a superhero and could have any power you wanted, what would it be and why?" The number one answer always seemed to be "being able to fly," followed by being invisible or having incredible strength or speed. Each one of those super powers had distinct advantages and enormous potential to help or harm!

Now when we ask adults what superpower they would choose, their answers move from self-focused to others-focused. Often, the answers change from flying, strength, and speed to powers that truly benefit others like healing, insight, and peacemaking.

If you could have any "superpower," what would it be and why?

And although none of us may ever experience those supernatural powers, we've all been blessed with incredible gifts and strengths; it's up to us to develop those "powers" and use them for the greatest good. But most of us will never even take the time to identify those strengths or the unique way we've been made.

In his best-selling book, *Now Discover Your Strengths*, Marcus Buckingham shows us the power of not only identifying our strengths, but leveraging them to live our best life. It's easy to see our weaknesses and we often spend an incredible amount of time and energy trying to fix our flaws. But we often neglect to focus on our strengths.

Identifying your unique gifts and strengths helps you define your power.

We believe that "Defining your Power" by identifying your unique gifts and strengths is the first part of finding your *Life Word* and living a life of positive impact.

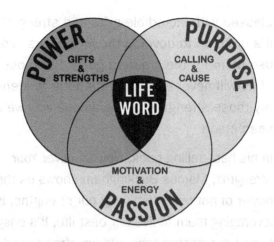

Some qualities you are naturally born with—we call these "gifts." Others are developed over time with effort and experience—we call these "strengths." Some of you were born with more compassion than others; maybe you've always cared about those who are getting the short end of the stick. Others may have been born with the "gift of gab" or the ability to communicate. Still others may have more patience or drive or energy. Some are born with more optimism and always see things on the bright side while others are more serious and cautious. Some can see the big picture while others love the details!

Some are more mechanically inclined while others are more creative or love nature. It's easy to see how God has wired each one of us in unique ways and it's a beautiful thing when we each utilize that for the good of others.

Gifts you are naturally born with; *strengths* you develop.

The best part of identifying your gifts and strengths is that it gives you clues about what you may be great at doing. If you're anything like us, you love living in your areas of giftedness and strength. Often that's the spot of your greatest performance and productivity. We love to be good at something; we love operating out of our strengths. It doesn't mean that we ignore our weaknesses or avoid stepping out of our comfort zone; not at all. Often our greatest learning and growth happens when we step out and take risks. But identifying our strengths helps us define those talents that are likely, if developed, to result in great impact and influence. It's all about leverage!

There are several questions we have found to help you to uncover your gifts and strengths. These are the top four questions to help you Define your Power: *What do you naturally excel at? What unique characteristics describe how you are naturally wired? What strengths have you developed over time? What gives you joy when you do it?* Asking a couple of close friends or family members what strengths or gifts they see in you can also provide you with insight into the way other people view you.

To prime the pump a little, here is a quick list of words that may describe you. Review the list and take a few moments to circle some words that you think fit you.

leading, administration, hospitality, compassion, serving, communication, belief, analytical, learner, teambuilding, organizing, simplifying, listening, encouragement, strategic, insightful, focus, visualizing, discipline, optimistic, patience, energy, positive, developing, building, creating, artistic, musical, writing, speaking, inventing, detail-oriented, vision, problem-solving, discernment, technology, teaching, training, empathy,

punctual, dreaming, dependable, honest, intui-
tive, motivator, work ethic, grit, perseverance,
resilience, joyful, tenacity, kindness, intellectual,
musical, confident, connecting, helping, humor,
networking, sensing . . .

The gifts and strengths that you circle and identify help give you clues to discover your *Life Word*. When combined with your purpose and passion, you gain more and more clarity on your way to leaving a positive mark on others.

chapter 6

Determine Your Purpose

Everything in life is designed and made with purpose. You are not an accident. You were made on purpose for a purpose because you have a purpose. Sometimes we immediately understand the purpose, and sometimes it takes time. But when you define your power and discover your purpose your life takes on new meaning and direction.

More people wrestle with this one question than perhaps any other—"Why am I here?" Put another way, "What am I made to do?" We believe that each one of us has been uniquely made with a purpose that we are specifically designed to fulfill. But often we get so consumed with some wildly "big" purpose that we miss all the "little" purposes along the way.

You are here for a reason.

Many have mistakenly bought into the deception that if they don't seem to have a big purpose like being on stage, starting a company, being famous, saving lives, or doing something heroic that their life is somehow insignificant and not that important. This could not be further from the truth.

In fact, it could be argued that our greatest purpose is to love God and love others. And, we can all do that. Every one of us can live on purpose every day, in big and small ways. It's often the accumulation of small actions that lead to a life of purpose and legacy. So instead of getting bogged down in trying to discover a purpose that is "bigger than life," let's approach our purpose from a little different angle.

Every one of us can live on purpose every day.

When we talk about purpose, we're really talking about what you can do to make a positive impact on others around you. We're talking about a sense of calling and investing in a cause.

Calling is when you have a sense of "I'm *made* for this!" It's when you find the thing to do that makes you feel most alive. Your Cause is found when you're able to say, "I'm *moved* to do something about this!"

Purpose is about a sense of *calling* and investing in a *cause*.

In what ways can you invest your gifts and strengths for the greatest good? What can you do to maximize your job and other opportunities to make a difference? After all, your job may not be your ultimate purpose, but it can be a vehicle to live and share your greater purpose. Living on purpose is about investing your life in the things that matter most so that you live a life of mission and meaning.

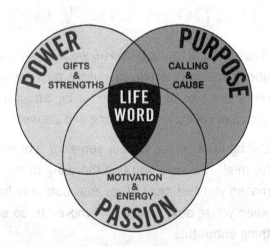

There's a well-known parable about "Talents." A wealthy landowner entrusts three of his workers with some money based on their abilities. To one he gave a "lifetime's" worth of money; to the second he gave about a year's worth of resources; to the last he gave about one month's pay. His instruction was simply to manage the money and give an account for what they did with it when he returned from his journey. The first two went right to work, investing the money and doubling it while the third buried it. When the landowner returned, he celebrated with those who had made the most of the opportunity, but took what the third man had buried and gave it to the other two.

It didn't matter how much each one started with; what mattered was what they did with what they started with. Did they live with a sense of purpose?

Howard Schultz, founder and CEO of Starbucks, is famous for saying "We're not a coffee company serving people; we're a people company serving coffee." He got it right. People are the object of their purpose—creating community and connections. Coffee is simply the excuse to get people together!

"Determine your Purpose" is the second part of discovering your *Life Word*. Purpose gives you a sense of direction and meaning. We believe your purposes are revealed by the one who created you. There are several key questions that we have found are helpful to reveal your calling and cause. These are the top five to help you Determine your Purpose: *What does the world need? What am I made to do to help fill this need? What can I do to make a difference and leave a positive mark? What breaks my heart? What's at risk if I don't do what I am called to do?*

Purpose gives you a sense of *mission and meaning*

Your purpose is ultimately something that frees you, challenges you, inspires you, and gives you a sense of mission and meaning. It's found by doing the things that make you feel most alive. So what is your purpose and how can you live and share it? When you can answer these questions, your life starts to make more sense.

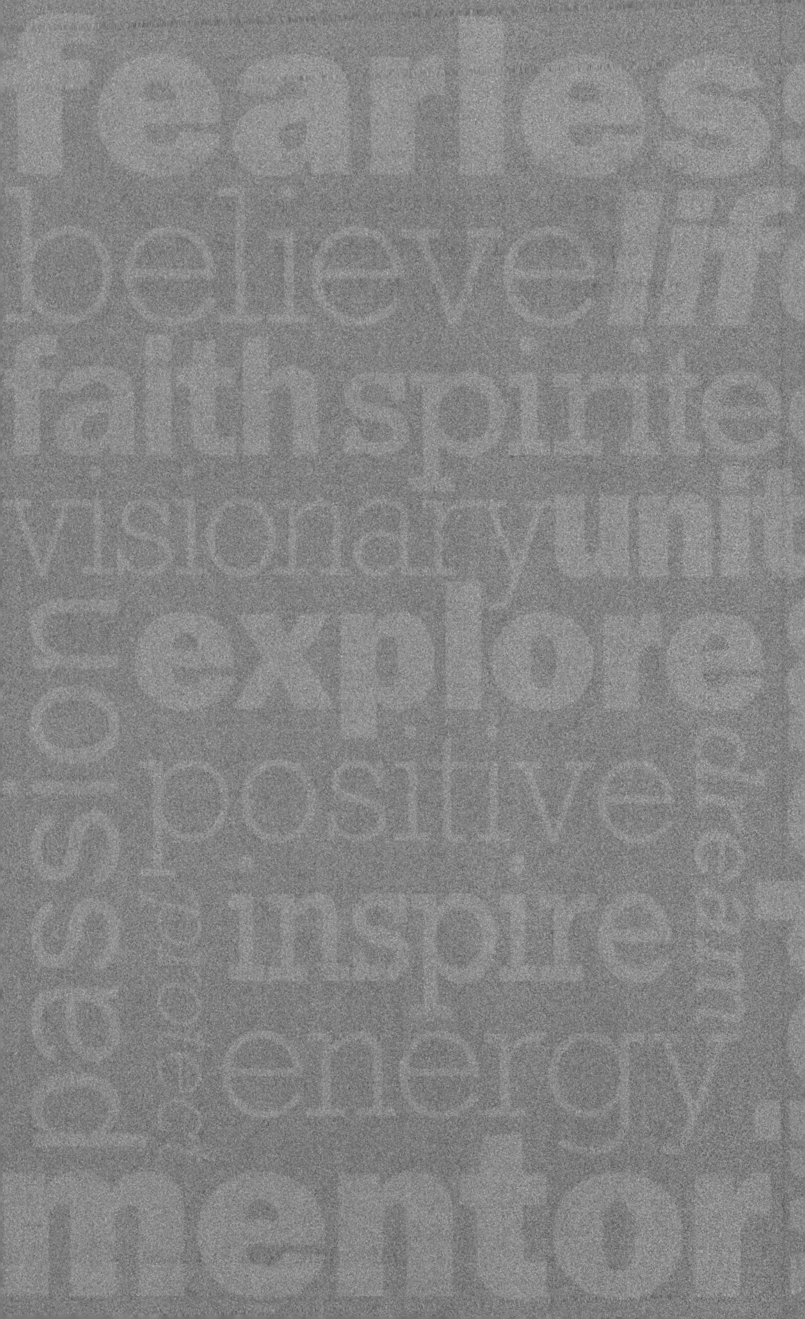
believe
faith
visionary
explore
positive
inspire
energy

chapter 7

Discover Your Passion

We've heard it said that passion is oxygen for the soul. It's also fuel for a life well-lived! We believe that nothing great can be accomplished without passion and enthusiasm.

It's easy to tell what someone is most passionate about! It's all about focus. Just take a look at three things—how you use your time, energy, and money. What we talk about most, spend our time on, and invest our money in reveals what we're most passionate about!

Passion is oxygen for the soul.

Think about it . . . we all know passionate people! We have friends who love the political season, who just can't wait to tell you who we should vote for! Others can't help but talk about their cars! Or maybe it's clothes or the newest technology upgrade or even online shopping. For some it's all about the next vacation or adventure trip.

Some are consumed by their work and can never shut it off. Some are driven by sports and they sacrifice every single weekend so they never miss a play. Others may have a cause that they are deeply committed to. Many of us are passionate about our families or kids and giving them opportunities to fulfill their potential. Some are passionate about giving back to their communities or helping others in need. All of these things are passions.

Passion is simply what drives you. It's what energizes you! It's what motivates you to take action. It's the force that gets you out of bed in the morning and keeps you focused to do your best.

Passion is what drives you, motivates you, and energizes you.

When passion is directed productively for the benefit of others, it can change the world for the better; it can give you the fuel you need to overcome obstacles and challenges, rebound from disappointment of failure, and fulfill your God-given purposes. Passion is filled with optimism and belief.

Passion is filled with optimism and belief.

Passion for things rarely satisfies. Passion for your selfish pursuits is rarely sustainable because it leaves you empty. But passion for others and the difference you can make in their lives is both sustainable and satisfying . . . and it leaves a legacy worth leaving. It gives you the chance to make the world a better place.

Passion is fueled by big dreams.

Martin Luther King Jr. had a big dream. He was passionate about equality. He was driven by social change that would lead to equal opportunity for all; that would ensure access to the American Dream that says we are all created equal and endowed by our Creator with certain inalienable rights to life, liberty, and the pursuit of happiness. But he was most passionate about changing minds and hearts, knowing that would be the catalyst for lasting change. He was a pastor and a civil rights leader. He dreamed that all people would be judged not by the color of their skin, but by the content of their character. He was passionate about having high moral character and conduct and then modeling it for others. He was driven to inspire others to take personal responsibility for their actions. He was energized by uniting all of us around his Dream.

Making a difference for others is the reason for great passion.

Passion is often driven by your conviction and energized by emotion. But passion is always about helping others and making a positive impact. When you're surrounded by people who share a passionate commitment around a common purpose, anything is possible.

"Discovering your Passion" is the third part of uncovering your *Life Word*. When you tap into your passion, it gives you the energy you need to live on purpose and maximize your power. There are several key questions that we have found

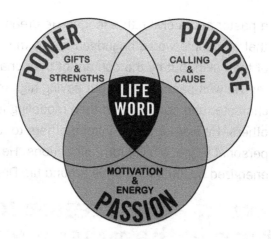

are helpful to reveal your motivation and energy.
These are the top three to help you Discover
your Passion: *Where do I invest most of my time,
energy, and money? What matters to me deeply?
What energizes me to take action and motivates
me to make a difference?*

Passion reminds you that what you're doing is
important. God plants seeds of greatness in
each of us and waters them with passion.

fearless
believe *life*
faith spirited
visionary unite
explore
positive dream
inspire future
energy wisdom
mentor

fearless
believe life
faith spirited
visionary unit
explore
passion
positive dream
inspire
energy
mentor

chapter 8

My
Life Word

Now it's time to discover your *Life Word*.

Your *Life Word* can be found at the intersection of your *Power, Purpose, and Passion*. We refer to this as the "sweet spot" or being "in the zone." No matter what stage of life you're in, your *Life Word* provides focus to help you live your best life.

Remember, your *Life Word* is meant to create clarity of direction and purpose to help you leave a positive legacy and make the world a better place. When your *Life Word* comes to you, it may be an action word, character trait, virtue, attribute, or even a value. The following examples of possible words are meant to be a starting point to prime your pump and give you an idea of potential words:

> *passion, inspire, positive, wisdom, potential,*
> *kindness, love, unite, builder, energy, life,*
> *spirited, hero, fearless, faithful, dream, strong,*
> *guide, trust, believe, balance, mentor, justice,*
> *fight, lead, bold, thankful, courageous, present,*
> *brave, teach, visionary, catalytic, encourage,*
> *joyful, smile, compassion, healer, pray, serving,*
> *protect, sacrifice, equality, relationships,*

> *humility, storyteller, peace, entrepreneur,*
> *connector, community, coach, influence . . .*

Some of these words might be a catalyst for your own discovery process. To assist you further, we've created the following action plan to help you prepare your heart and discover your *Life Word*. These five steps will help you get clarity and focus.

Step 1: Preparing Your Heart Is All about *LOOKING IN*

Take a little time to unplug from the busyness, noise, and distractions of life and create an environment to look in, quiet your mind, and really listen to your heart. We believe this process invites God to speak to you.

In each of the three circles—*Define your Power, Determine your Purpose,* and *Discover your Passion*—words or themes will start to "bubble up" to the surface. These words will act as clues as you seek to discover your *Life Word*. Take a few moments now to revisit the answers you gave to the questions in each step. List some words from each step here.

Define your Power by answering the following questions:

1. What do I naturally excel at?
2. What unique characteristics describe how I am naturally wired?
3. What strengths have I developed over time?
4. What gives you joy when you do it?
5. What strengths or gifts do your close friends or family members see in you?

List your gifts and strengths here:

_____

_____

Determine your Purpose by answering the following questions:

1. What does the world need?
2. What am I made to do to help fill this need?
3. What can I do to make a difference and leave a positive mark?
4. What breaks my heart?

5. What's at risk if I don't do what I am called to do?

List your calling and cause here:

_____

_____

Discover your Passion by answering the following questions:

1. Where do I invest most of my time, energy, and money?
2. What matters to me deeply?
3. What energizes me to take action and motivates me to make a difference?

List what motivates and energizes you here:

_____

_____

Step 2: Asking Your Inner Circle for Insight Is about *LOOKING AROUND*

We have also found that it can be incredibly helpful to invite those who know you best to speak into the process. Choosing people who you trust that may know you in a couple of different capacities is particularly helpful.

Ask two or three people from your inner circle—those who know you best—to give you insight by asking:

> Is there a single word that you think helps define who I am and what my life is all about? What's One Word that you think of when you think of me? A word that captures the difference I have or will make in the world? What impact have I made on your life?

Give them permission to brainstorm a little bit and come up with two or three words so they don't feel the pressure of getting the "perfect word" right off the bat.

List those potential words here:

_____

_____

_____

Step 3: Beginning with the End in Mind Is about *LOOKING AHEAD*

In Chapter 2 we challenged you with one simple question—"What will people say about me at my funeral?" If family members, friends, and co-workers were to stand up at your funeral and share about you, what would you long for them to say? What impact will you have made? What mark will you have left behind?

Jot down a few thoughts and reflections here:

_____

_____

_____

Step 4: Discovering Your *Life Word* Is All about *LOOKING UP*

Now that you have prepared your heart, reviewed the steps, and received feedback from your inner circle, you are ready to receive your word.

As we mentioned in Chapter 2, your *Life Word* gives you a guiding hand to make sure that you live on purpose, align your priorities, and live with passion to make a difference for others. It acts as a lighthouse of sorts to help you stay focused on the things that matter most.

As men of faith, we look to our Creator to receive our word. We believe there is a *Life Word* that's meant for you. That's why, in a room with hundreds of people, almost everyone will have a different word. It's a word that captures who you are, why you're here, and what drives you. It captures your hopes and dreams mixed with your gifts and talents. It helps you live well and leave a legacy that you are designed to leave— a legacy that will change the world and make it better in some important way. We encourage you to boldly ask God for your word; be willing to listen and be patient. Listen for God to speak to your heart and reveal your *Life Word*.

So let us be your "life coach" right now. Put your *Life Word* on your tombstone right now and evaluate how it fits. Is that the mark you want to leave? Is that what you want to be known for? Is this the title of the story that God wants to write in your life? By doing this exercise, your word will become very clear. You may have to try out two or three words to get the right word and that's a good thing! Give it a shot right now.

My *Life Word*

_____

Step 5: Living out Your *Life Word* Is All about *LOOKING OUT*

Once you discover the word that is meant for you, it's time to use it to live on purpose, exercising your gifts and talents fueled by what motivates you. It's time to keep your word front and center. Here are a few suggestions to help you maximize the effectiveness of your *Life Word:*

- Create a *Life Word* journal. Put your *Life Word* on the cover and utilize it to capture memories, moments, and milestones.
- Paint a *Life Word* picture. If you aren't a gifted artist, buy a picture that reflects your *Life Word*. Place it where it can be seen every day.
- Buy a large rock or stone for your garden. Write or engrave your *Life Word* on it. You can go into your garden and stand on the rock and meditate, reflect, or pray. It will be a reminder that your *Life Word* is your foundation of your life.
- Write a poem, story, song, or prayer about your *Life Word*. Don't keep it private. Share it with others.

- Create a *Life Word* wall at home or work. Your *Life Word* can be centered on the wall with your yearly One Words around it.
- Name your pet or child after your *Life Word*. (Okay, that might be a bad idea.)

These are just a few of the ways you can keep your *Life Word* front and center. Have fun with your *Life Word* and be creative. The sky is the limit!

chapter 9

It's Never
Too Early
(or Too Late)

Now that you have discovered your *Life Word*, we want to encourage you that it's never too early—or too late—to begin building your legacy. We realize that depending on what stage of life you may be experiencing, the idea of leaving a legacy may come with a heavy sense of responsibility, a nagging sense of regret, or even a heightened sense of urgency.

It ought to be the business of every day to prepare for our last day.

—*Matthew Henry*

For those who are young and just starting out in life, this focus gives you an incredible advantage for your journey. It will help you make wise decisions and maximize your opportunities along the way. But don't get weighed down by your word; instead, use it as a catalyst to be your best. Use your word to help you discover God's path for your life, develop your strengths, and live with a sense of destiny.

When they were just 18 years old, brothers
Alex and Brett Harris published their first book,
Do Hard Things. With that, they also sparked a
revolution, or "rebelution" as they like to say,
that challenges teenagers to rebel against the
low expectations of our culture, do hard things
to make a difference, and glorify God. This
movement at therebelution.com has sparked
countless stories of young people attempting
and achieving great things for the good of others and to make the world a better place.

We also know that our lives often may be
changed in many ways. Our purpose sometimes
hits us like a lightning strike and we have a
eureka moment where everything becomes
clear. Other times our greatest adversity
becomes the catalyst for our new and greatest
purpose.

When Bethany Hamilton was just 13 years old,
a rising star in the sport of surfing, she lost her
left arm in a shark attack. For many people,
that might have ended their dream of surfing
professionally, but not Bethany. Her determination and grit coupled with the incredible sup-
port of her family propelled her back into the

water just one month after the attack and then on to becoming one of the greatest female surfers in the world. She turned her adversity into a life that through her books, speaking, and movies inspires people to overcome fear and obstacles. She is building a legacy of passion, perseverance, and hope.

Because life brings changing seasons and circumstances, we want to let you know that your *Life Word* may change over time. Don't feel like you're stuck with the word you select now. We encourage you to reflect on your *Life Word* and reevaluate it every 10 years. In his twenties Jon would not have picked the word "positive." But by his thirties, it was clear. We have found that our *Life Word* helps us live our purpose and our purpose helps us choose our *Life Word*. As our purpose sometimes changes, so will our *Life Word*.

For those near the "half-way" point on your journey, this focus may be just what you need to reorient, reprioritize, and reinvest your time, energy, and resources around the things that matter most! It may also reinforce the path you are on! But be careful not to get bogged down with a sense of what could've or should've been; instead, put the past behind you, learn from it, and move on with a sense of renewed purpose and energy.

Dean Karnazes rediscovered his passion for running at age 30. At an early age, Dean loved running, and when he entered high school he began to show potential with long-distance running. However, his high school track coach sucked the joy out of running for him, so he stopped running altogether. On his 30th birthday, he experienced an epiphany and was gripped by desire to run once more. After hanging up his running shoes for 15 years, he took off into the night and ran 30 miles. This experience reignited his love for running, and he has become one of the top ultramarathoners in the world and was named by *Time* magazine as one of the World's 100 Most Influential People. It was in his third quarter of life that his passion was rediscovered and gave him a clear purpose.

And for those in the "fourth quarter" of life, this focus will help you maximize your wealth of life experience and pass on wisdom to the next generation. It may even help you repair relationships, overcome regrets, and finish strong. Use your renewed sense of urgency to focus and fuel you to make a difference for others. Right now, you may just be positioned to do the greatest good as you run with endurance and finish the race!

In 1888, Alfred Nobel was mourning the loss of his brother Ludvig when his grief was magnified. He'd just read the obituary in a French newspaper, but it wasn't his brother's . . . it was his! An editor had confused the brothers and wrote the headline, "The Merchant of Death Is Dead." Alfred Nobel's obituary described a man who had gotten rich by helping people kill one another; after all, he was the inventor and producer of dynamite. Shaken by this appraisal of his life, Nobel resolved to use his wealth to change his legacy. When he died eight years later, he left more than $9 million to fund awards for people whose work benefited humanity. We know these awards as the Nobel Prizes. Alfred Nobel had a rare opportunity—to look at the assessment of his life at its end and still have the chance to change it. Before his life was over, Nobel made

sure he had invested his wealth in something
of lasting value. He finished well.

We want to share two personal experiences
that demonstrate it's never too late to make a
difference and leave a legacy.

Dan's Mentor

For more than 20 years, I had a mentor named
Barry Spofford, a retired naval captain who
served for 30 years. Barry and I worked together
for the Fellowship of Christian Athletes for
many years. As someone who was 20 years my
senior, I had great respect for his wisdom and
insight. Every time we met, he challenged and
encouraged me to confront the challenges and
celebrate the wins.

Early in his Navy career, Barry experienced several major losses. His first wife died of cancer,
and losing his wife was followed by several more
personal tragedies. In his early forties, he hit
rock bottom and slipped into deep depression.
Through a series of events, he was lifted from
the depths of despair to a newfound faith. In

this season of life, he discovered the power of prayer.

Barry passed away in 2015, but his legacy lives on. For the entire second half of his life, he was known as a man of prayer. Prayer for him wasn't a last resort but his first response. Thousands of people have been marked by Barry's *Life Word*. His *Life Word* impacted his own life and the lives around him. He taught me that prayer is the foundation to life. Barry's *Life Word* was **Prayer**.

Jimmy's Mom and Dad

I recently had a wonderful conversation with my mom on her 78th birthday. I asked her what she thought her *Life Word* would be. Of course, she began to tell me that she didn't think she had accomplished much in life, that she didn't really have any notable gifts or strengths—it was classic Mom! A certain level of sadness seemed to be creeping in as she thought about what kind of mark she made and the legacy she would leave behind. I could tell she also felt like she may have wasted time and was now "running out of time."

So I took the opportunity to share with her the things I admired about her and the impact that she had, especially in raising me and my siblings. I voiced some of the things that I would probably say at the end of her life. Her spirits immediately lifted and she was ready to really consider the One Word that might tie her life together.

She then revealed her *Life Word*—**Kindness**. I sat there stunned because that was the exact word I would have chosen! Anyone who has ever encountered my mom would say the same thing! She spreads kindness, never having a negative word about anybody. We could trace the positive and lasting effects of her kindness in our family, in her marriage of more than 50 years, and beyond. And I think it energized her to live with more purpose, passion, and power going forward.

I had a similar opportunity with my dad. As I challenged him to look back on his life at the things that he was most passionate about, the things that brought him energy and life, and the mark that he made in the lives of others, the

Life Word **Teach** became obvious. In fact, it was the first word that came to him. And it most clearly defined his path! Not only was it uplifting to his spirit, but it also has the potential to refocus his energy and attention as he makes the most of his years ahead!

No matter where you are on life's journey, your *Life Word* will help you live with more determination and clearer direction as you live out your God-given destiny. It's never too early or too late to start!

fearless
believe *life*
faith spirited
visionary unite
explore
positive
inspire
energy
mentor

fearless
believe
faith
spirit
visionary
explore
positive
inspire
energy

chapter 10

Now
What?

Now it is your turn to put your *Life Word* into action!

Life isn't a sprint or a 5K run. It is a marathon that gives you plenty of time to internalize your *Life Word* and integrate it into every dimension of your life. In our first book, we share six dimensions to incorporate your One Word:

1. Physical
2. Mental
3. Spiritual
4. Emotional
5. Relational
6. Financial

You can do the same with your *Life Word* and apply it to all six dimensions. When you do, you'll live your best life—the life you've been made to live and share with others.

Remember, your *Life Word* doesn't guarantee success; life is full of ups and downs. The promise of it is a life of meaning and mission—not perfection. Your *Life Word* will equip you to maximize every day no matter what the day brings. It will help you rise to meet your challenges, remembering that there's purpose even in pain. Living your *Life Word* is one of the most rewarding but challenging things you will experience. It sharpens and refines you. You will become the person you are meant to be.

Life is too short and precious to not live it to the fullest. Don't let fear keep you from your destiny. Don't let apathy keep you from experiencing an exciting and meaningful journey. Live your *Life Word* with faith and courage and make a profound, positive difference in the lives of others and leave the world a better place. Can you imagine if you and I and all of us live out our *Life Words*?

- Families will be strengthened and united.
- Homes will be safe places full of joy.
- Relationships will be healed and restored.
- Schools will be full of kids realizing their potential and finding their path to greatness.
- Businesses will be fueled by integrity and positive energy.
- Communities will be safer and more connected.

The positive impact we all would have together could literally transform the world. So let's do this together. Let's discover and live out our *Life Words* and go leave a lasting legacy!

GetOneWord.com

One Word has already changed thousands of lives. Now it's your turn. We have produced free resources to help you do that. These resources will help you put your *Life Word* process into practice.

- Share your *Life Word* story and pictures.
- Download *Life Word* posters.
- Make *Life Word* presentations.
- Sign up for our free newsletter.

Acknowledgments

The One Word journey can be summarized in one word—**Miraculous**. We had no idea that a simple concept in 1999 would impact hundreds of thousands of lives around the world. This miracle would not be possible without our family, friends, and all the One Word fanatics out there. Though we can't thank everyone, we would like to recognize the following people:

- The John Wiley & Sons publishing team. Thank you for challenging and encouraging us to write book number two. Special thanks to Matt Holt, Shannon Vargo, Elizabeth Gildea, Peter Knox, and Deborah Schindlar.
- Our Heavenly Father who not only gives us our One Words each year but also abundant life through the gift of Jesus. We are three men who are simply saved by grace and for that we are eternally grateful.
- Dan would like to thank Dawn, Kallie, Abby, and Eli, who have believed, supported, and loved him since day one. He would also like to thank Jimmy and Jon for running the race

of faith with him. He is a better man of God because of you.

- Jimmy would like to thank his wife, Ivelisse, and their four kids—Jimmy, Jacob, John, and Gracie. They are his love and passion and continually make him strive to be his best. They will be his most prized legacy.
- Jon would like to thank his wife, Kathryn, and children, Jade and Cole, for loving and supporting him as he has struggled and learned to live out his *Life Word*. He would also like to thank Dan and Jimmy for inviting him on this life-changing One Word journey with them. He knows he's a better man because of their friendship and the books they've written together.
- All the One Word believers who have been using and spreading the concept for years.

About the Authors

Jon Gordon is a best-selling author and keynote speaker whose books and talks have inspired readers and audiences around the world. His principles have been put to the test by numerous NFL, NBA, and college coaches and teams, Fortune 500 companies, school districts, hospitals, and nonprofits. He is the author of *The Energy Bus Wall* (a *Wall Street Journal* bestseller); *The No Complaining Rule*; *Training Camp*; *The Shark and the Goldfish*; *Soup: A Recipe to Nourish Your Team and Culture*; *The Positive Dog*; and his latest, *The Seed: Finding Purpose and Happiness in Life and Work*. Jon and his tips have been featured on *The Today Show*, CNN, *Fox & Friends,* and in numerous magazines and newspapers. His clients include the Atlanta Falcons, Campbell Soup, Wells Fargo, State Farm, Novartis, and Bayer, among others. When he's not running through airports or speaking to businesses, hospitals, or school leaders, you can find him playing tennis or lacrosse with his wife and two high-energy children.

You can e-mail Jon at **info@jongordon.com**. Follow him on Twitter at **@JonGordon11**.

 **Dan Britton** is a speaker, writer, teacher, coach, trainer, and marathoner. His passion is to help people live intentionally, maximize relationships, and invest in the next generation. As a lacrosse fanatic, he has played and coached lacrosse for more than 40 years and even played professionally with the Baltimore Thunder. He has coauthored five books including *One Word That Will Change Your Life*, *WisdomWalks*, *True Competitor*, and *Called to Greatness*; and also authored and edited 12 additional books. Dan's been interviewed by national outlets like FOX News, CBS News, and Fast Company. In his role as the international executive vice president with the Fellowship of Christian Athletes, he travels extensively around the world training thousands of coaches and

athletes and works with more than 60 countries. He is married to his high school sweetheart; and yes, all three of his children play lacrosse. They reside in Overland Park, Kansas, and have three grown children: Kallie, Abby, and Elijah.

You can e-mail Dan at **dan@fca.org**.
Follow him on Twitter at **@FcaDan**.

 **Jimmy Page** is a speaker, author, trainer, leadership coach, and Spartan racer. He is passionate about investing everything he has by inspiring others to live their best life. He invests in businesses, sports teams, schools, and non-profits around the world to create healthy, high-performing cultures that make a positive impact. He has coauthored six books including *One Word That Will Change Your Life*, *WisdomWalks*, *True Competitor*, *Called to Greatness*, and *PrayFit*. Jimmy has been featured on FOX NY, CBS News, Fast Company, Janet Parshall's America, and in numerous magazines and on radio shows. As a lifelong athlete and competitor, he's also a NIKE

Sports Performance Coach and the featured guest on the *FitFridays* radio program. He and his wife started an innovative cancer organization called BelieveBig.org following her victory over cancer. He builds leaders and teams as a vice president for the Fellowship of Christian Athletes. Jimmy is married to his college sweetheart and they reside in Maryland with their four amazing kids—Jimmy, Jacob, John, and Gracie.

You can e-mail Jimmy at **Jimmy@jimmypage.us**.